How to Discipline a Toddler

A Parent's Essential Guide to Disciplining Toddlers, Dealing with Toddler Tantrums, and Addressing Other Toddler Behavior Problems

by Patricia Munsford

Table of Contents

Introduction

All parents face the colossal task of teaching discipline to their toddler. Without your guidance, a toddler has no concept of what is right or wrong. Lacking physical, psychological, mental, and emotional maturity, he is ill-equipped to deal with frustrations and changes to his known routine. He has no concept of boundaries, and in his limited way of looking at things, he's determined to have what he wants, when he wants it. And at this age, a toddler's inability to maturely articulate the presence of unmet needs leads to tantrums.

How you deal with your toddler's outbursts is a matter of personal choice, but if you want to learn positive ways of teaching discipline to your toddler, you've come to the right place! This book will help you to better understand your toddler, the reasons behind his tantrums, how you can prevent them, and how to handle them when they do occur. This book is also geared towards helping parents effectively teach their child about self-control.

Armed with the knowledge contained throughout the pages of this book, you will no longer be the helpless parent in the mall shouting at your son to stop throwing things, or pleading with him to stop screaming. Instead, with the assistance of these positive approaches to discipline, you will be able to easily maintain control of the situation while remaining cool, calm, and collected.

Chapter 1: Teaching a Toddler Discipline

Children that have been taught discipline at a very young age turn out to be obedient, respectful, and dutiful kids. Such children become well-balanced individuals because at a very early stage in their life, they have learned about self-control, respect, and proper conduct. Parents bear the responsibility of teaching discipline to their children and the best time to start doing that is when the children are still young. That way, discipline becomes an integral part of their foundation as a person. And while some parents of toddlers may choose to delay teaching discipline until a later age, it remains essential that toddlers learn discipline.

Teaching toddlers discipline can be quite a challenge as kids in this early stage have no real concept of what is right or wrong. Nevertheless, parents of generations before us have done it and you, the parents of today can certainly do it. Using the following tips, the task can be effortless, straightforward, and uncomplicated. Understand and practice these helpful guidelines and in time, it would be child's play to discipline your toddler.

Setting Rules and Limits

Parents of toddlers need to set certain limits. Those who failed to do so will have to live with the thought of having raised spoiled children. Teaching discipline to your toddler starts with you creating rules that you and your toddler can stick to. For instance, all parents know that too much chocolate or ice cream is bad for your kid's teeth and general health. Does that mean then that you will deprive your child of ice cream and chocolate throughout his childhood? No. It means that you will have to teach your young child that he can only eat limited amounts of these foods. The challenge lies in how you can make a toddler understand this simple rule and make him abide by it. Also, parents must be able to keep the rules they make and not just give in to the demands of a bawling toddler. Otherwise setting rules and limits becomes useless when the toddler sees that the adult cannot implement them. Parents of toddlers need to understand that the rules they make and the limits they set are not created to restrict their child but to protect him from possible danger or harm. This is the reason why parents need to be strict in implementing the rules and limits that they set for their young kids. Many times, a toddler will want to test whether the same rule still applies and so parents need to remain firm.

By creating rules for your toddler, he learns what things are allowed and what are not. Rules teach a child about self-control and abiding by rules gives him an opportunity to strengthen his willpower. Moreover, setting limits allows your child to learn the valuable life lesson that he cannot have everything he wants just because he cries. Another reason why parents need to set limits is that the child will actually feel much safer with boundaries that his parents have set for him. For instance, parents tell their child all the time not to stay near the edge of the stairs because he could fall, not to go beyond the fence because it's dangerous, not to climb up high places, and so on. Over time, young children learn that the limits that their parents have set are actually there to protect them. This makes them feel safe. There could be a number of reasons why some moms and dads are unsuccessful at setting limits for their toddlers. It includes the lack of ability to be firm when it comes to their toddler's demands, they can't tolerate to see their child crying, or they simply don't know how to implement the rules they made without resorting to hitting.

Letting Your Toddler Know Who Is in Charge

One mistake that some parents make is allowing their toddlers to become their masters. They follow everything that their child says and give in to his every demand. This is the opposite of teaching discipline. A toddler needs to know that you are the adult and that between you and him, you are the one who's in charge. How many times have we seen a child throwing a tantrum in the grocery, toy store, or park just because he cannot have what he wants? My father-in-law skips feeding my three-year old daughter her breakfast and lunch just because she announces that she is not hungry. Clearly, the adult is the one following the toddler. Adults know what is right or wrong, proper or improper. Toddlers do not. Therefore, a toddler should never be given the power to make decisions, especially about issues concerning his health or safety. If you let your toddler decide what to have for lunch, he will choose ice cream. Remember that your being in-charge protects your toddler from any possible harm.

But how to teach your young child about authority is another gigantic challenge that every parent must face. Always keep in mind that hitting and verbal abuse is never an option. Shouting will only show your child that you are not mature enough to use effective communication. One effective way to teach your toddler about your authority is to allow him to make mistakes. Parents always provide instructions to their young sons and daughters but a normal toddler will do as he pleases. And when a bad consequence happens, the child realizes that his parents were wiser than him and that he should heed their words. For instance, when you instruct your toddler not to jump up and down on the sofa and if he ignores your words, just keep on reminding him that he could fall down and hurt himself. Let him learn the lesson by allowing him to make the mistake. Of course, make sure that your child is never in real danger. When he falls and feels the pain, he will remember that you told him not to do what he did. He will recognize that your instructions are for his own good and that you, as his parent, know what is best for him.

Discipline and Self-Control

Disciplining your toddler is never about controlling him. Keep in mind that your goal in teaching discipline to your tot is so that he can have the ability to control himself. And while fathers and mothers need to show their authority over their young kids, keeping this goal in mind can help to teach discipline more effectively. Every mom and dad should do all that they can in order to help their toddler attain this goal.

The Importance of Structure

Young children need to feel secure in order to develop into well-balanced individuals, and one way to give your toddler this precious feeling is by creating a safe and stable environment for him. While there are many ways to make your tot feel secure, one of the most effective ways is to create structure for him. Structure gives reassurance to your young child that he is not in danger. For instance, setting a daily routine schedule for your toddler can be very helpful to his development because he becomes familiar with it, and in time, he will be able to complete each task safely and easily. This will also help develop his self-confidence. Creating structure for your child allows him to focus on maintaining good behavior and it also keeps him away from danger.

Chapter 2: Positive Approaches to Discipline Your Toddler

How many times have we seen a mother yelling at her toddler to stop yelling? Parents always fall for the trap of teaching their kids one thing and setting as example the exact opposite of what they're trying to teach their kid. I have seen a mom hit her child because the toddler hit another kid. How can a mom teach her son that hitting is bad by also hitting him?

Truly, there is nothing more challenging than disciplining a toddler. Nevertheless, it is essential and all parents need to do it. So how can moms and dads discipline their young child without hurting their child, getting a sore throat, and elevating their blood pressure? The answer is to choose the positive approach. Here are positive, effective ways to help you better discipline your child.

Step 1: Say No To Shouting and Hitting

First of all, stop shouting yourself and never even consider hitting your child. These confrontational methods are never effective in teaching your child about self-control. These harmful ways can negatively affect your toddler emotionally, physically, and mentally. The damaging effects can be long-term and even permanent. So if you catch yourself raising your voice, stop talking right away. Instead, you should practice communicating with your child more effectively. Sit him down and speak to him in a normal voice. If you are angry, leave the room and regain your composure before having a talk with your child.

Step 2: Understanding Your Toddler's Behavior

It would help parents take care of their toddler better if they made an extra effort to understand their child's behavior. Your toddler will not just act out without any significant cause. Why is your tot behaving that way? Is he hungry, tired, sleepy? Does he need attention from you? Perhaps, he needs to use the potty. Find out the reason for his actions. By doing so, you can help your child behave better.

Step 3: Work on Controlling Yourself

You are the parent, the adult and should never let a toddler dictate how you should react and behave. Toddlers will do anything and everything because they have not reached full emotional and mental development. Therefore, we cannot blame toddlers for their behavior. On the other hand, you are responsible for all your actions. So as a positive approach in disciplining your toddler, practice being more patient and more understanding of your little one. Always make an effort to control your temper.

Step 4: Reinforce Good Behavior

Let your toddler know that you are happy with his good behavior. Be generous in giving praises and in rewarding good conduct. For instance, if you visited a friend's house and your toddler showed good behavior throughout the visit, tell him how proud and happy his good behavior made you feel. Simple rewards such as a kiss on his cheek, a hug, or a new book can go a long way in reinforcing his good behavior.

Step 5: Spend Time with Your Child

A lot of parents become too busy with work, household chores, and other stuff that they don't take the time to sit down and play with their toddler. Young children need the physical, mental, and emotional presence of their parents. Some parents are in a hurry to send their child to nursery school so that they can have more time for themselves. The toddler years are numbered and if parents don't treasure this point in their child's life, they'll never get the chance again. The strong presence of a parent provides the child with a feeling of security and this can help him develop confidence. Moreover, toddlers need constant care, attention, and guidance from their parents.

Chapter 3: How to Avoid Toddler Tantrums

Toddler tantrums are common and even the most behaved child will throw a tantrum given a good reason. What we all need to understand is that child tantrums are natural. A tantrum is a child's way of expressing himself, although, we all agree that it is not the best way. So, what parents need to do is to teach their child the proper way to express himself. Tantrums are natural but they can be prevented. Here are some effective tips to prevent a toddler tantrum.

Step 1: Give Your Toddler the Attention He Needs

The most effective way parents can prevent a toddler meltdown is to pay attention to the needs of their child. Moms and dads that are too busy chatting with friends, doing housework, browsing on their iPhones often miss the signs leading to a tantrum. Remember that tantrums are already the extreme way of communication for toddlers. And toddlers don't just go into tantrums for no reason. Pay attention to your child and don't ignore their needs. When a toddler's needs are met, such as food, sleep, warmth, comfort, and the need for the parents' attention, then there is no reason for a toddler to have a tantrum.

Step 2: Keep Toddler Schedules

Young children rely on fixed schedules that make them feel safe and comfortable. Any change in their usual schedule can trigger a tantrum. My three-year old child follows a strict sleeping routine in order for her to sleep soundly at night. We do this around the same time every night. One evening, we had some friends over and I let her stay awake past her sleeping time. Naturally, she had a meltdown that resulted to a very upsetting situation. Parents need to strictly keep the schedules that their young kids are used to, especially when it comes to feeding and sleeping time. Toddlers become grumpy when they are hungry, sleepy, tired, and want to use the potty. Therefore, if you want to prevent a tantrum, don't take your child shopping when it's his nap time and don't allow him to keep playing when it's time to eat.

Step 3: Ready Your Toddler for Changes

In the event that you are unable to keep your toddler schedule, prepare your child for any changes. For instance, if you and hubby have to be away for the weekend and your toddler will be sleeping at grandma's home, then take all possible actions to prepare him for this. Talk to your toddler and explain that mommy and daddy will be away for a couple of days, so grandma will be the one to look over him. You should help your child adjust to the new situation as best as you can. Perhaps you can pack his favorite toys and even his own pillows and blanket so that he won't be too shocked with his new environment. You can lessen the chance for toddler tantrums when your child knows what to expect. Young children will feel threatened by anything that they are not familiar with, so help your child understand beforehand any changes in his routine.

Step 4: Be Firm but Flexible

You know that you have to be firm about your toddler rules and limits. However, there are times when you have to use your better judgment as a parent. For instance, your rule is no snacks before meals. However, if you are caught in traffic on your way home and won't be able to make dinner time, will you let your child starve in the car just because of this rule? I certainly hope not. Parents need to be able to implement rules but they should also know when rules are just rules. Keep in mind that toddler rules are created to protect and not to cause harm.

Step 5: Offer Choices

Many times, your toddler will insist on what he wants. The best way to handle this situation is to offer him choices that are actually better for your child. For instance, your 4-year-old daughter wants you to buy her a very expensive doll and you just don't have the money for it. What can you do? Drag her out of the store screaming and endure the looks from other people as she throws a tantrum? You can try offering her another alternative such as two cheaper toys, a book she always wanted, or an ice cream cone instead. As a parent, you know your child best, so dig into your memory and remember another thing that your child might want instead of this very costly doll. This strategy is effective not only because it helps a parent get out of an awkward situation but also because the child feels that she is given control over a situation. She will appreciate being given the ability to decide instead of just always doing what her mom or dad says.

Chapter 4: Dealing with Toddler Tantrums When They Occur

So what can parents really do when their toddler is already in a full-blown tantrum? What parents need to understand about tantrums is that it does not happen without a reason. Due to a toddler's inability to express himself adequately, he resorts to crying and outbursts. Still many parents believe that a toddler is behaving this way in order to manipulate the adult, but this is not true. Instead, a toddler expresses his frustration when his needs are not met through tantrums. Here are helpful ways to handle your child's tantrum.

Step 1: Stay Calm

It's not helpful to lose your cool whenever your child loses his. Instead, make an effort to remain calm. Your child may shout, whine, kick, and even try to hit you but you have to stay calm. When this happens in public, don't feel pressured to do something right away just because people are looking. Stand over your child and work on controlling yourself. Don't feel embarrassed by the situation because that can trigger your own anger. Ignore the other people and focus on your child only.

Step 2: Hug Your Child

Whenever my three-year old daughter throws her once-a-month tantrum, I gather her in my arms and try to hug her. She will struggle for a few minutes, will try to get away, or hit me but I offer her comforting words and I never take my arms off her. In less than five minutes, she stops struggling and is all calmed down but is still crying. Hugging your child will help him calm down and it will also prevent your child from hurting himself during his tantrum.

Step 3: Talk to Your Toddler

After my toddler has calmed down a bit, I ask her what made her upset. Usually, she will tell me the reason behind her tantrum. I get rid of the cause and assure her that everything is okay now. Many times, I see parents that command their toddler to stop crying without finding out what caused the child to feel upset. If you are not aware of the cause of the tantrum, the best way to find out is to talk it out with your tot.

Step 4: Meet Your Toddler's Needs

As soon as you find out the real cause of your toddler's tantrum, then you can address it accordingly. Parents need to find out the reason so that they can give the appropriate solution. If the root of the tantrum is not removed and the child's attention was just diverted, then he could feel upset about the same thing all over again. For instance, if a tot is hungry, he should be given food. Distracting him with toys may temporarily stop him from crying but it will not solve his problem which is hunger. A sleepy toddler will need sleep and a sick child will need care and attention.

Parents must be able to respond accordingly to their child's needs and in order to do that, the parents need to find out and remove the cause of the tantrum. In case you have no power to remove the cause, you still have the power to remove your child from the environment that is upsetting him. For instance, if you are at a very noisy place and you deem that the loud sound is the cause of your child's tantrum, then leave the place and take your child to a quieter, more comforting place. If it's another person that is making your child upset, then take your toddler away from that person.

About the Time-out

A time-out is described as letting your toddler be whenever he is having a full-blown tantrum. You don't approach him or talk to him, but instead, just let him cry it out and allow him to freely express his anger and frustration. Many promote this method, but I personally think that it is ineffective and could even be harmful to the child.

Humans need response from other humans. We feel happy, assured, and comforted when there are other people that listen to us, look at us, respond to us, and are aware of our existence. Being ignored is the worst kind of punishment, in my opinion. When people don't look at you, don't listen to you, don't acknowledge your presence, and intentionally ignore your existence, that is the worst feeling in the world. The effect can be very damaging to any human being.

Every person needs attention and human response, but especially a young child. In my experience, the time time-out is not a productive way to discipline a child. It makes the child feel alone and the no-action from his parents can have a damaging effect on the child's trust for his parents. Remember that young kids need to feel safe all the time. Responding to their cries is one way to assure toddlers that they are safe and that there are people looking out for him.

Nevertheless, the use of time-out in disciplining toddlers is widespread and is supported by many parents. If you wish to try this disciplinary method, then that is your prerogative as a parent. However, I encourage you to read more about it and also to ask your pediatrician about its effectiveness. Just remember though, that all children are unique and one method of disciplining can be effective for one but not for the other. Your child is also a unique individual and so, you must choose the disciplinary style that works best for you and your child.

Chapter 5: What **NOT** to Do When Disciplining a Toddler

All parents develop their own styles to make their toddler behave. Some rely on tried-and-tested methods of disciplining their child while others resort to more unconventional ways. However, some of these non-traditional ways could actually be doing more harm to your young one. Here are disciplinary styles that every parent must avoid.

Don't Bribe

When toddlers are bribed by their parents, they learn to associate good behavior with rewards and therefore, they come to expect rewards every time good behavior is required of them. Consequently, that good behavior comes only with a reward, and they may even stop reacting with good behavior once rewards are not given.

Don't Lie

Lying to toddlers just to make them behave and do your bidding will have dire consequences later on. It is best to be always truthful to your child and if that is impossible, at least don't make a habit of telling big lies to your toddler. Also, at some point, your child will find out that you were not telling the truth and that can negatively affect the way he responds to you disciplining him. And while it's very tempting to use white lies, it is still best to stick to facts and reality when dealing with a toddler.

Don't Give Ultimatums

Young children need to see your authority as their parent. It makes them feel secure to know that there are mature, responsible, knowledgeable, authoritative people around them. However, when you make ultimatums to your child such as telling them to eat their food or the monster will come and get them, they will want to test your threat. A toddler who does not want to eat will close his mouth and although scared, he will want to see if what you said is true. So he'll wait for the monster and when no monster comes, he'll know that your words are empty.

Don't Play Good Cop, Bad Cop

Do you and your partner play the "good cop, bad cop" when disciplining your toddler? Even if it works, your child's relationship with the parent that plays the "bad cop" may eventually suffer. Both parents need to be the "good cop". Every toddler must be able to feel safe with both parents and not just one of them. Also, children look up to their mother and father and will expect only the good from both of them.

Don't Be Divided

When disciplining a toddler, the mother and father need to have a united front. Once your child sees any weakness in any one of his parents, he will use this to get what he wants. Therefore, parents need to talk before creating rules, setting limits, giving rewards or implementing punishments. Plus, they have to agree on everything, otherwise the toddler will sense that one parent does not agree and he will take advantage of this.

For instance, if the rule is that the child can only have one scoop of ice cream, then both parents need to be firm about implementing it. If one parent backs down and gives the toddler another scoop, then the rule is broken and the other parent's authority is undermined. For the child to learn discipline and recognize both parents' authority, moms and dads need to stick together.

Furthermore, a parent should never say anything to a toddler that disparages the other parent. This will only confuse a young child and can affect the way he regards the parent who disses and the parent being dissed.

Don't Set High, Unreasonable Expectations

Your child is a toddler. What were you really expecting from a child aged 2, 3, 4, or 5? Praise your child for achievements and good behavior. Allow him to make mistakes that he can learn from. Don't put pressure on your very young child to be something that he isn't ready for yet. Treasure your child in his young age. Let him be a toddler.

Chapter 6: Knowing When to Seek Professional Help

My neighbor has a 16-year old son with Down's syndrome. Piolo has the body of a ten-year old and the mind of a five-year old. Coming from a family with low economic status, the child is unable to study and have access to all his needs. Many times, I see him having a tantrum right in the middle of the street and no one is able to help him, not even his mother. I have also seen a video of a mother and her son with ADHD. She wants to share with the public her struggles as she tries to teach her child discipline. In these cases where the child has a learning impediment, a mental condition, or a personality disorder, the parents will need the help of medical professionals.

The advice given in the previous chapters are for parents that face the common problems of raising toddlers, meaning toddlers who have no mental disability or personality disorders. If you suspect that your child is not developing normally, have your doctor check your toddler. Children with mental retardation or some personality disorder will not be able to learn discipline as efficiently as the average child. If your child has a mental condition or a personality disorder, you will need the professional assistance of your doctor in order to better help your child learn about self-control, proper conduct, the concept of authority, and so on.

When your child is throwing tantrums and you are unable to pacify him no matter what you do, it is advisable that you consult with a medical practitioner to find out whether his tantrums are normal or not. Especially in the cases where your child hurts himself, either or both of his parents, or his siblings, immediate action must be taken. Today, therapists and pediatricians are easily able to identify any warning signs that your toddler may be mentally challenged or have a personality disorder. The sooner your child gets the professional help he needs, the better his chance of leading a disciplined, if not a normal life.

Conclusion

The toddler years are, perhaps, the most memorable for every parent. Who can forget the cute, chubby faces, the adorable giggles, and those monstrous tantrums? Every parent has been through a full-blown tantrum. Many have learned to effectively deal with it while others are still struggling with their little ones. Tantrums can be physically and emotionally draining for both the parent and the child. Parents don't want to see their little ones crying and suffering and some will not know what to do in these situations.

I have seen the many, different ways moms and dads handle their bawling toddler. Some are quick to discipline by hitting, more are inclined to shouting, and a lot just allow their child to roll all over the floor until they become tired. I, too, am a mother of a toddler and I have tried various ways to handle my child's tantrum. The most effective method for me is to hug her and to talk to her. I have discovered that your keyword when dealing with your child's tantrum is to "comfort".

In this book, I have explained to you that tantrums are a child's way of communicating his anger or frustration. Therefore, a parent needs to comfort the child, to assure him, to help him. Parents should never shout, hit, or ignore a child who is having a tantrum. This is the child's cry for help. So the next time your child is having a fit, go to him, comfort him, and meet his needs. Once your child realizes that you are always there for him and that you are able to address his needs, he will feel secure, safe, and assured that he has a reliable guardian. Your toddler will be able to fully trust you as his parent. All of these positive feelings are crucial when teaching discipline to a very young child.

Toddlers will always be prone to tantrums for these are natural. They will also demonstrate other behavioral problems as they grow. However, parents need to remember that toddlers are acting this way because they are not emotionally and mentally capable to do otherwise. Hence, parents need to treat their toddlers with patience and understanding. Moms and dads out there should also remember to regularly assure their tantrum-prone little one that they love him very much, no matter what.

Finally, I'd like to thank you for purchasing this book! If you found it helpful, I'd greatly appreciate it if you'd take a moment to leave a review on Amazon. Thank you!